L
for t

Susan Hardwick

First published in 1997 by
KEVIN MAYHEW LTD
Rattlesden
Bury St Edmunds
Suffolk IP30 0SZ

ISBN 0 86209 965 X
Catalogue No 1500101

0123456789

Cover photograph courtesy of Images Colour Library Limited
Cover design by Jaquetta Sergeant

Edited by Janet Payne
Typesetting by Louise Hill
Printed and bound in Great Britain

CONTENTS

FOREWORD

This little book is intended for those who are experiencing a troubled relationship of one sort or another, or who are coming to terms with its consequences.

Each one of us is on a series of journeys through life. There is the major journey from birth through to death, and beyond; the shorter journeys through the various stages of our lives, and the journey taken through each major event.

Each journey contains within it different stages or processes, and the amount of time needed to go through each stage will vary from person to person. You may not yet have reached the third or fourth stage for the first time – or you may be re-covering ground you have already trodden: things we think we have come to terms with at one level of our understanding often have to be worked through again at deeper levels before we can truly say that healing has taken place. Whatever stage you are at, I hope you will find comfort, encouragement and hope in reading these prayers, reflections and meditations.

May the God who is closer to us than we are to ourselves, bless you on your journeying.

SUSAN HARDWICK

PROLOGUE

Once,

a wounded man
stumbled,
fell,
and knew
the depths of despair,
the wells of loneliness.

He allowed this
to happen to himself
in order to show
the rest of humankind
that he understood
what it was
to drink such dregs.

His
name
is
Jesus.

WAYS TO PRAY

The first thing to say is that there is no one set way to pray, nor one set sort of prayer; the variety of prayers in this little book is an example of that.

There is just one, cardinal, rule: we must always try to be totally honest in our prayer; to speak it just the way it really is – whether it is a shout of pain, anger or bewilderment, a cry of joy and thanksgiving, or a request for ourselves or for someone else.

As individual and unique people we each have an individual and unique relationship with God; as unrepeatable as is our own set of fingerprints. In just the same way, our prayer relationship with God will be unique.

Prayer, in fact, begins with God and not with ourselves.

'You did not choose me,
no, I chose you . . .' says Jesus. *John 15:16*

God is constantly praying in us, speaking to us, and softly knocking on the door of our heart. When we feel the urge to pray, we are answering this invitation. It is a bit like responding to a softly, but insistently, ringing telephone.

It is very important, though, that we do not do all the talking, and so prevent God from getting a word in edgeways. It is a good rule of thumb that, like a telephone conversation, we should not do more than fifty per cent of the speaking. Once we can get in the habit of listening to God, most probably we will often find it very surprising what he has to say to us.

Prayer is both the easiest, and the hardest, thing in the world. Hard because it demands honesty and commitment; and easy, because it is like coming home to an infinitely loving parent. And, like such a parent, we can be confident that we can say whatever we feel at the deepest part of our being, and that whatever we do say will be understood and valued. Like anything worthwhile, it does need working at if we are going to get deeper and deeper in our relationship with God – but the pay-off can be amazing, and totally life-changing.

One way to begin is just to open our mind and heart, and to say exactly how we feel in all its rawness and honesty. To lay it all out before God, then to ask him for his understanding and wisdom, his strength and healing, to come into those things and situations; and for those same qualities of

God – wisdom and strength, and so on – to be his gift to us.

It is hard to concentrate our minds, and to pray, when our bodies are restless. If that is so for you, do try the following:

Sit in a comfortable, supportive chair, with legs uncrossed and hands resting in your lap. Close your eyes and concentrate first on making your breathing steady and even. Now work your way down your body in your mind, beginning at the top of your head and concentrating on each area. Any area in which you notice tension imagine as a block of ice, a knotted rope, or a coiled spring. Then imagine it melting, unravelling, loosening. Return to your breathing. As you breathe in, think the word 'Jesus'. As you breathe out, think the word 'me'.

This, in itself, is a prayer.

Now you are relaxed, just listen to what God wants to say to you in the silence of your heart. If you want to speak to him, do so.

Another creative way to pray is to take a few words of Scripture which are meaningful to you, to do the relaxation as above, then to let the words dwell in your mind and sink into your heart, allowing their deeper meaning to speak uniquely to you and your situation.

You could use your imagination. Let it roam as wide and wild as it likes. Picture any situation, of your own or in the wider world. Or take a passage from one of the Gospels. Imagine yourself there. Picture yourself and Jesus together in the situation. What do you say to him? What is he saying to you?

God can be found in all things; for example, a photo, a picture, a lit candle, an object that you look at or hold, newspapers, can all be aids to getting yourself into prayer.

For Jesus, prayer was a way of life. Being rooted in prayer gave him the knowledge of God's will, the wisdom, the direction, the strength and the courage that he needed.

Prayer can be the same for us too, if we let it.

Protest and Pain

God urges us to be absolutely honest in our dealings with him: to say it just the way it is, how it feels, for us.

Jesus cried out from the Cross, at what must have been the darkest time of his life:

> 'My God, my God,
> why have you forsaken me?'
> *Matthew 27:46; Mark 15:34*

His prayer gives us the example, the courage, the openness to be just as honest about our feelings: to say, to shout, to scream, maybe, it all just the way it really is.

Lonely

I'm so lonely, Lord!
Inside of me is an aching void
as deep, and as wide,
as the world.
Please show me how to fill it.
Amen.

Betrayed

Oh, Lord – how *could* he leave like that!
Don't our years together matter at all?
One minute we seemed to be fine;
the next – everything had changed.
I feel so humiliated and betrayed;
reduced to less than nothing.
I just want to crawl away
and hide from the world.
I don't want to bear other people's pity.
Give me back my sense of self-worth.
Amen.

Bewilderment

Dear Lord – how the years have flown!
And now these old bones
get tired so very easily.
But do advancing years
have to mean extra loneliness?
Little by little, as the time has passed,
the family remember me less and less
and I'm so bewildered by their lack of care.
I know their days brim over
with a great variety of activities,

whereas mine are filled
with increasing emptiness.
But how very dearly I would love
a visit,
a phone call
or even a little note.
Dearest Lord, please grant me my wish.
Amen.

Broken

Broken promises,
broken dreams,
and a broken heart.
Gather up these shattered fragments, Lord*
these pieces left of my heart, my life,
so that they are not all wasted,
and graft them into your own.
Amen.
* John 6:12, 13

Despair

When did that sweet-natured child
turn into this hard-voiced stranger?
We used to be so very close

– but now a chasm lies between us
as wide as the world.
Whatever I say, whatever I do,
I just cannot seem to get through.
Is this the way it is going to be
from now on?
Sometimes I feel on the edge of despair.
Help me, Lord. Inspire me.
Show me what I should do;
tell me what to say.
Amen.

Hate

Dear God!
I hate her!
I *really* hate her.
Please help me!
Amen.

Injustice

Why me, Lord?
Why us?
What have I done
– let alone the children –

to deserve all this?
You're supposed to be
a God of Justice.
So, why did you
allow this to happen?
Amen.

Mum and Dad . . .

Oh, Jesus, Mum and Dad:
they're going to split!
They're *so* selfish. What about *us*?
Didn't they think what it'd do
to our lives as well?
They want us to choose.
But we love them *both*.
Please make it the way
it always used to be
– before the arguing began.
Amen.

Secret love

The love which framed my life,
and filled it with richest meaning
is one that I can't talk about

to any other than you, Lord.
It was – is – a love
that dares not tell its name,
and that's what makes the pain
so very much harder to bear.
I cannot sustain much longer
this terrible pretence, this outward facade,
that nothing whatever is wrong
– whilst, inside, my heart is breaking.
Dear God, give me someone to talk to.
And please don't you desert me
in my desperate need.
Amen.

Together – but miles apart

We're still together, Lord,
yet miles apart in every way.
I'm far more alone like this
than if I was on my own.
Please show me what to do.
Amen.

COMFORT AND CONSOLATION

God is always with us. Unseen, unfelt maybe, nevertheless closer to us than we are to ourselves. Throughout the Bible, again and again we are assured of this fact.

> Come to me all you who labour and are
> overburdened and I will give you rest.
> *Matthew 11:28*

With these words, Jesus assures us of his loving and constant care, wherever we are and in whatever situation – but never more so than when life is hard, when we are in despair, when we cannot go on in our own strength.

The Old Testament

> Do not be afraid, for I am with you;
> do not be alarmed, for I am your God.
> I give you strength, truly I help you,
> truly I hold you firm
> with my saving right hand.
> *Isaiah 41:10*

As a mother comforts a child,
so I shall comfort you . . .
Isaiah 66:13

Be brave, take heart,
all who put your hope in God.
Psalm 31:24

God said:
'I myself shall go with you
and I shall give you rest.'
Exodus 33:14

God is a stronghold to me,
my God is my rock of refuge.
Psalm 94:22

God lifts up those who are bowed down.
Psalm 145:14b

I waited, I waited for God,
then he stooped to me
and heard my cry for help.
He pulled me up from the seething chasm,
from the mud of the mire.

He set my feet on rock,
and made my footsteps firm.
He put a fresh song in my mouth . . .
Psalm 40:1, 2, 3a

The New Testament

When the Lord saw her,
his heart went out to her
and he said, 'Don't cry'.
Luke 7:13 (NIV)

Blessed be the God and Father
of our Lord Jesus Christ . . .
who gives every possible encouragement;
he supports us in every hardship . . .
Just as the sufferings of Christ
overflow into our lives;
so too does the encouragement
we receive through Christ.
2 Corinthians 1:3, 4a, 5

God, who encourages all those who are
   distressed . . .
2 Corinthians 7:6a

Look, I am with you always;
yes, to the end of time.
Matthew 28:20b

Peace I bequeath to you,
my own peace I give you,
a peace which the world cannot give;
this is my gift to you.
Do not let your hearts
be troubled
or afraid.
John 14:27

The Lord is near.
Never worry about anything,
but tell God all your desires
of every kind
in prayer and petition
shot through with gratitude,
and the peace of God
which is beyond our understanding
will guard your hearts and your thoughts
in Christ Jesus.
Philippians 4:5b-7

HOPE AND HEALING

If we are honest in our dealings with God, somehow trusting and hoping even when things appear hopeless; if we listen to his reply and open ourselves up to his healing touch, then gradually the wounds of anguish and fear will begin to knit together and, one day, we will be able to declare ourselves healed.

May the God of hope fill you with all joy
and peace as you trust in him,
so that you may overflow with hope
by the power of the Holy Spirit.
Romans 15:13 (NIV)

Jesus made them welcome and talked to them
about the kingdom of God; and he cured
those who were in need of healing.
Luke 9:11

You stayed close

Thank you, Jesus,
for staying close beside me
through that terrible time.
Amen.

Time heals

They say, don't they, Lord,
that time is a great healer:
and so it is proving for me.
Although I still have dark days
when sad memories predominate,
there are more and more bright ones
when I remember the good times, too.
Thank you, Lord,
for putting back the balance.
Amen.

You gathered up the fragments

When it happened, Jesus,
I prayed to you
to gather up
the shattered fragments*
of my life, my heart,
and to make me whole again.
I don't really think
I believed you could.
But I underestimated you,
and your skill at mending.

Today, when I look at me,
I can scarcely see the joins,†
and I know I'm stronger than before.
Amen.
* *John 6:12* † *Jeremiah 18:3-5*

When Mum and Dad split . . .

When Mum and Dad decided to split
I thought I should die
with the pain and the hurt of it.
But now I can see
how much happier they are.
So,
perhaps it *was* for the best,
after all.
Thank you, Jesus,
for being there
when I so needed you.
Amen.

Perhaps it was the best thing

I could see no rhyme
nor reason at the time.
But now?

Perhaps it was the best thing
– after all.
Thank you, Father,
for helping me to see it.
Amen.

Someone to confide in

A blessed miracle, Jesus!
You sent me someone to talk to.
Someone to whom I can unburden my heart
without any fear of betrayal.
How true it is
– I myself have proved it –
that a sorrow shared
is indeed a sorrow halved.
Thank you, Lord!
Oh, *thank you*.
Amen.

The hate has gone

One day it was there.
The next, the hate had gone.
Thank God! I'm free of it.
Amen.

We've begun to talk

Heavenly Father,
I prayed for the right words
to reach out to my son;
and you gave them to me.
It wasn't much of a conversation,
but at least it was a beginning.
Help me, help us both to build upon it,
and to re-create our relationship.
Amen.

The rainbow begins with me

The end of the rainbow
has always been somewhere else.
But today I looked up
and saw it began at my feet.
A celestial pathway leading
straight to you, Heavenly Father.
Now I shall no longer fear
journeying on my own.
Amen.

LOOKING FORWARD

It is usually fear of what the future will bring which prevents us from looking forward; but there comes a time when we have to turn from the past in order to contemplate, to affirm and to embrace the future. We have to turn the boat around, so to speak, and, instead of rowing, face the way we are going and paddle.

It happened that one day Jesus got into a boat with his disciples and said to them, 'Let us cross over to the other side of the lake.' So they set out, and as they sailed he fell asleep. When a squall of wind came down on the lake the boat started shipping water and they found themselves in danger. So they went to rouse him saying, 'Master! Master! We are lost!' Then he woke up and rebuked the wind and the rough water; and they subsided and it was calm again.

The calming of the storm: Luke 8:22f.
See also Psalm 107:28-30

Whole again

Most holy Lord –
That blessed day has finally come;
at last I can say I'm truly healed.
Thank you for making me whole again.
Amen.

Always there

Most loyal friend and Saviour;
you were with me
in the dark times,
and will be
in all the times ahead.
Amen.

I hoped in God

'Hope in God!'*
That's what you told me.
And that's what I did
– and it has made
all the difference in the world.
Amen.
* Psalms 42-43

Peace at last

Blessed calm, at last!
Oh, Lord, I can't tell you
how very good it feels
no longer to be tossed about
by that storm of emotions.
Thank you, Jesus,
for this sense of peace.
Amen.

A turning to the future

I thought I'd cried
all the tears in the world,
and still they came.
But with them
there is a cleansing,
and a healing,
and a letting go
– and a turning
to the future.
Thank you, Lord,
for holding me
during it all.
Amen.

New relationships

Heavenly Father –
I look to the future,
and new relationships,
with confidence
and with excitement.
Amen.

I still so wish . . .

I still so wish they hadn't split,
and we were all together
– like it was before,
when we were small.
But, if it can't be like that then
I guess this is the next best thing:
they're so much happier
now they are apart.
I still find it hard,
and it still hurts
– but it's getting better.
At least I can count on you, Jesus;
you'll never let me down.
Amen.

Standing in the twilight

Watching the sun set tonight,
rose-tinting the distant horizon
with gigantic streaks of finger-painting
trailing the colours across the sky,
I felt the beauty of your Creation
through every fibre of my being.
 Such a beautiful vision
called out the sadness,
replacing it with gladness
and hope for the future.
Thank you for opening my eyes
and making me see beyond myself.
Amen.

May God bless you

For so many years
– almost more than I can recall –
we have travelled through life together.
But now our paths must diverge.
It's clear to see you have set out
on a journey that excludes me.
It's a journey that you have decided
you want to make alone;
upon which I can't accompany you
– and at first that hurt so much.
I too will have to learn new ways
when you are gone:
to see life through two eyes once more,
and not four.
May God bless both of our travelling,
and may he make your
– and my –
paths straight.
Amen.

Epilogue: Paul's Prayer

This, then, is what I pray,
kneeling before the Father,
from whom every fatherhood,
in heaven or on earth, takes its name.
In the abundance of his glory may he,
through his Spirit,
enable you to grow firm in power
with regard to your inner self,
so that Christ may live in your hearts
through faith, and then,
planted in love and built on love,
with all God's holy people
you will have the strength to grasp
the breadth and the length,
the height and the depth;
so that, knowing the love of Christ,
which is beyond knowledge,
you may be filled
with the utter fullness of God.
Glory be to him whose power,
working in us, can do infinitely more
than we can ask or imagine.
Amen.

From the *Letter to the Ephesians*